~Craft Ideas for Your Home~

STENCILING

~ *Craft Ideas for Your Home* ~

STENCILING

CANDIE FRANKEL

Little, Brown and Company
Boston   New York   Toronto   London

To Jean

Acknowledgments

The author gratefully acknowledges the many fine photographers and

designers whose work is featured in these pages and professional stenciler Debbie Gideon,

who shared her expert instruction with uncommon grace.

First edition

ISBN 0-316-29168-4

Library of Congress Catalogue Card Number 94-77001

A FRIEDMAN GROUP BOOK

10 9 8 7 6 5 4 3 2 1

Published simultaneously in Canada by Little, Brown & Company (Canada) Limited

CRAFT IDEAS FOR YOUR HOME: STENCILING
was prepared and produced by
Michael Friedman Publishing Group
15 West 26th Street
New York, New York 10010

Editor: Elizabeth Viscott Sullivan
Art Director: Jeff Batzli
Designer: Lynne Yeamans
Layout: Ed Noriega
Photography Editor: Colleen Branigan
Production Associate: Camille Lee
Illustrator: Barbara Hennig

Printed and bound in China

Contents

Introduction

Stenciling is the craftsperson's answer to four white walls yearning for decoration. Easy to learn and readily mastered, stenciling can reflect virtually any decorating tradition. Designs can be realistic, abstract, historical, geometric, or country-style. Hues can be muted, for a soft watercolor look, or deep and rich, for striking contrast. Used sparingly, stenciling can accent architectural features, such as a gabled window or an arched passageway. Used lavishly, stencils can pattern walls, floors, and ceilings.

Successful stenciling depends upon pattern repetition; a pattern may be simple, but gains "momentum" when duplicated and arranged over a surface. A basic square, for example, can be stenciled many times to create a checkerboard. A simple vine can grow into a sinuous border that rambles around a room. Many richly decorated surfaces can emerge when different stencil designs are grouped together and second- and third-color overlays are introduced. Unlike the perfectly spaced, identical patterns on commercial wallpaper, stenciling offers room for variation, playfulness, and personal touches.

For those who confess to having little artistic ability or inclination, stenciling is a made-to-order craft. Designs are easily adapted from readily available sources, and the actual stenciling process is logical and can be approached step by step. The art that emerges from this straightforward, methodical labor astounds everyone, every time, with its living beauty, rhythmic pulse, and handcrafted appeal. The rest of this introduction is devoted to the steps and tips that will make your stenciling projects a success and help you re-create rooms as vivid and as exciting as those featured in the photographs throughout this book.

Understanding Stenciling

Stenciling is an ingenious technique that has been in use since antiquity, and its wide range of applications has included borders inside Egyptian tombs, inscriptions in medieval chapels, and lettering on twentieth-century shipping crates. The prime reason to choose stenciling to embellish a surface is speed. Rather than drawing and painting motifs individually, which could take many hours of concentrated work, the stencil artist uses a single cutout stencil to transfer the same image many times over. When paint is brushed over the stencil, the surface that is exposed through the cutout area receives color, but the areas that are blocked by the stencil do not.

To prevent the paint from seeping beyond the cutout edges, the stencil material must be waterproof. Historically, stencils have been cut from oil-saturated paper and cloth, waxed paper, and leaves (the ancient Egyptians used papyrus). Stencils cut from these materials remained sharp and clear for only a limited number of images before they had to be replaced. Twentieth-century technology has

Opposite: Stencils used to point up architectural features are most effective when they are slightly larger than the feature itself. In an elegantly furnished front entry hall, the rolling spiral stenciled above the chair rail is particularly noteworthy because of its depth. Ascending the staircase is a combination feather-and-dot border that parallels the deep woodwork above it. The white wall space carved out between the two borders became the perfect niche for a framed theorem painting, a type of stenciling on velvet that was taught in young ladies' academies in the early to mid-1800s.

introduced Mylar polyester film, which is easy to cut, is virtually indestructible, and has the added advantage of being translucent, which makes for easier tracing and alignment.

Materials and Equipment

A STENCILING CHECKLIST

• Paints
• Brushes or natural sponges
• Stencils
• Paper plates
• White artist's matte tape
• Dressmaker's chalk
• Plumb line
• String
• Powdered chalkline
• Retractable metal ruler
• Triangle or T-square
• Retarder
• Lighter fluid

Your stenciling checklist will look something like the one above. The first five items are necessary for all projects, while the items toward the end of the list are discretionary—you can decide whether or not they will be useful to you.

The most important stenciling purchase is paint. Before you can choose colors, you must decide what type of paint to use. The key characteristic to consider is the paint's drying time. The stenciling technique requires that paint be applied sparingly, so that it doesn't run or drip beyond the cutout edges, and that it dry quickly, so that you don't have to wait

long intervals before you can lift the stencil and move on to the next motif. When you align a stencil on top of previous work to continue a border or to add a new color, the paint underneath must be dry enough so that it does not smear.

The two main paint choices for stencilers are acrylic paints and japan paints. Acrylic paints are widely available and are very popular for general craft use. They are water-based and quick-drying, and brushes, sponges, and stencils can be washed clean with soap and water. For stenciling projects, however, acrylics can be difficult to work with. Because acrylics do dry so quickly, it is very difficult to keep the scant amount of paint needed for stenciling from hardening on the brush. The "window of opportunity"—the time when the brush is dry enough for proper stenciling but moist enough to be workable—is very small. Some stencilers overcome this problem by using retarder, a commercial product that mixes in with acrylic paint to prolong the drying time. Others find it easier to apply acrylics with a damp sponge instead of a brush.

Japan paints, which are oil-based, are the choice of many professional stencilers. Unlike most oil-based paints, which typically dry very slowly, japan paint contains a special fast-drying agent similar to that used in lacquers. Some stencilers squirt a few drops of lighter fluid into each glob of japan paint they use to accelerate the drying even further. Like all oil-based paints, japan paints must be cleaned with a solvent, such as mineral spirits or paint thinner. Beginners often avoid japan paints solely because they envision a messy and prolonged cleanup process, and they miss out on the joy of working with beautiful, jewel-like colors

that practically lay themselves on the walls. Brushwork is quick and easy with japan paints, as the oil content helps keep the bristles damp,,pliable, and perfectly loaded with color. Overall progress is quite rapid, too; generally, a pattern can be stenciled on a surface for two or three running feet (0.5 to 1m) before it becomes necessary to work new color into the brush.

Both acrylic paints and japan paints come in a variety of colors. Acrylic colors can turn opaque and chalky-looking, and the stenciled motifs may appear slightly raised on the surface. Japan colors have a delicate translucent quality, and the paint is thin and lies flat on the surface. Since so little paint is used in stenciling, a standard two- or four-ounce (56 or 112g) container of craft acrylic paint or an eight-ounce (224g) can of japan paint will take you a long way. Other options for stencilers include oil sticks, which generally dry overnight, metallic enamels, and gold leaf and other metallic papers.

To apply the paint through the stencil, you will need brushes or sponges. Stencil brushes are round and squat, and the bristles are evenly trimmed. You can use either synthetic or natural bristles with acrylic paints, but japan paints are best applied with natural black boar's hair bristles. A broad brush about one inch (2.5cm) in diameter will make your work go faster. It helps to have a separate brush for each color, especially if you are using japan paints. That way, you won't have to interrupt your stenciling to clean your brush when you're ready to change colors. For smoother stenciling with acrylic paints, you may want to try substituting natural sea sponges for brushes. Elephant ears—the small sponges used by potters during wheel throwing—are handy for detailed areas.

Stencils can be purchased ready-cut or you can cut your own by hand (see page 10). Craft, art-supply, and home-decorating stores stock a variety of precut stencils from established designers that can be used for walls, floors, furniture, and textiles. Many beautiful, intricately cut designs are available. If you're timid about combining patterns, try three or four from a single designer's line—they will be coordinated and are guaranteed to work well together. Another source worth checking is a quilt-supply store for the stencils used to transfer quilting patterns. Designed for stitching, these patterns can yield unusually delicate borders, medallions, and trellis effects.

Precut stencils are handy if you are itching to start stenciling right away, but they do have drawbacks. Crisp, precise machine cuts can cause stenciled work to appear static and lifeless. Commercial stencils are generally smaller than those you can cut yourself, which means you have to reposition them more frequently to stencil the same surface area. Many stencils marketed today tend to repeat the same themes and to borrow ideas from one another, which limits your decorating choices. For designs that truly express the interests and personality of your household, handcut stencils offer many more options for just a little extra effort.

The two remaining "must-haves" on your stenciling checklist are paper plates and white artist's matte tape. Ordinary white paper plates (uncoated, with a rippled edge) make perfect palettes for the small amount of paint you will use. If you are stenciling correctly, you should use no more than half a dozen dinner-size plates per room. The tape is used to secure the stencil to the wall or floor surface while you stencil. White artist's tape is recommended

because it peels up more easily than masking tape and will not mar the surface finish. Uses for the remaining supplies are discussed in the sections that follow.

Designing and Cutting Stencils

~

- Design source
- 5-mil (0.125mm) Mylar polyester film
- Mechanical pencil
- Ruler or straight edge
- Drafting template with circles
- X-Acto craft knife
- Plate glass (at least ten inches [2.5cm] square) with masked edges
- Permanent fine-tip marking pens in assorted colors

Cutting a stencil for a particular room is a thrilling first step toward achieving a decorating goal. Take time to fantasize about the type of design you would like (this book will help spur your imagination) and try to find its look-alike in a book of actual-size stencil patterns. Many books about stenciling include patterns, ready for tracing, that readers are free to use. Other design sources are printed fabrics and wallpapers, children's books, needlework designs and borders, illustrated art and architecture books, and posters. If the design you want is a bit out of the ordinary, look for any photograph or illustration that you can copy as a simple line drawing. Remember, a stencil has no shading and no crisscrossed lines. There are only two types of spaces on a stencil: the areas that are cut away, and the areas that remain solid.

To prevent the stencil from becoming too flimsy, large or long areas of an image—a tree trunk, for example—may be represented by smaller sections linked by bridges. A bridge is an area of the stencil material that is not cut away but is deliberately left intact to add strength and stability. It is best to have all of the bridges the same width and length to avoid calling attention to them. The more you study stencil design, the better your grasp of bridges will become.

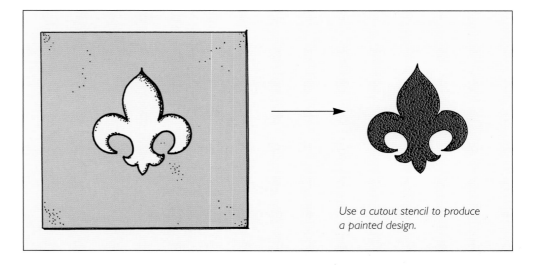

Use a cutout stencil to produce a painted design.

Bridges add stability without interrupting these willow branches' graceful arcs.

10

Once you have chosen a usable, actual-size pattern, your next step is to transfer it to Mylar polyester film. Mylar film is sold at art-supply stores by the sheet and on rolls. Buy film in the 5-mil size (0.005 inches [0.125mm] thick) that is cloudy on one side only. Lay the film on the pattern, cloudy side up, allowing a minimum three-inch (7.5cm) margin all around. Using a mechanical pencil so that you always have a sharp point and your lines are of equal width, trace the pattern lines directly onto the film surface. If the pattern includes any small circles or straight lines, draw them using a drafting template or a straight edge. Make your drawing as perfect as you can.

To cut the stencil, lay the film, cloudy side up, on a square of plate glass. (Make sure the edges of the glass are masked with tape to prevent cuts.) Use an X-Acto craft knife with a sharp blade to cut all the marked lines. To cut straight lines, run the blade along a straight edge or ruler. To cut curves, hold the knife steady and rotate the film away from you. Try not to lift the blade from the surface in the mid-

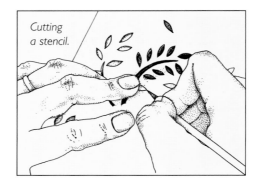

Cutting a stencil.

dle of a long stretch to assure a more fluid curve. Points and corners will be crisper if you extend each cut slightly beyond the end of the marked line.

One advantage to cutting your own stencils is that you can use film sheets as large as you wish. A commercial pattern eighteen inches (45cm) long may be able to fit only two motifs, while a handcut stencil thirty-six inches (1m) long can fit four of the same motif. The longer the stencil, the longer the section of wall or floor you can cover in one pass. To prepare a long border stencil, trace the motifs as many times as will fit, making sure the spacing between them is uniform. Work carefully, but do not be overly concerned about making the images identical. The small variations that your hand tracing and cutting bring to each motif will add a distinct, handcrafted quality to your work.

When you have finished cutting a long border stencil, you should test it and add permanent register marks. To do so, tape several large sheets of paper together and lay the stencil on top (A). Transfer each outline with a pencil. (If you have your paints out and ready, you can stencil with paint instead.) When the entire stencil image is copied on the paper, slide the stencil to the right so that the right edge of the paper image flows into the left edge of the actual stencil. Measure to confirm the spacing between motifs. Taking care not to shift the stencil from this position, trace a few key shapes from the paper image onto the Mylar film using a permanent fine-tip marking pen (B). Repeat this process on the other side by sliding the stencil to the left. Even though you can see through the film, these register marks will give you extra assurance as you

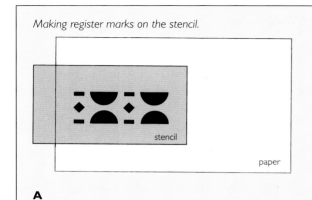

Making register marks on the stencil.

A

transferred previously · cutout section of stencil

stencil

trace outlines for register marks

B

stencil with cutouts and register marks

C

stencil that everything is perfectly aligned. Marking both sides (C) will let you continue your stencil in either direction.

Many stencil designs call for two or more colors. To create these, you will need to draw and cut a separate stencil for each color. The colors generally appear side by side in the finished design, but sometimes one color is superimposed on top of another. Most tracing patterns in stencil books are printed in black only. If you have trouble visualizing such a design in color, make a tracing on paper and fill it in with colored pencils. You can use your colored tracing as a guide when you cut the stencils. Follow the same test procedure used for borders to make permanent register marks on each stencil in the set.

Applying the Color

~

Using your stencils to decorate a room is quite easy—most people can hardly wait to see what their designs will look like. Place a small thumbnail-size glob of paint on a paper plate palette, and if you choose, mix in retarder (for acrylic paints) or lighter fluid (for japan paints). Dip the end of the brush into the paint mixture, then swirl the brush in a circular motion on a dry area of the plate to coat the tips of all the bristles and to work off the excess paint. When the brush is almost dry, it is ready for stenciling.

Before beginning to paint, make sure the stencil is taped securely in position. Work the brush in a circular motion over all the cutout areas of the stencil. Do not labor too long in any one spot: keep moving on to new areas. Hold down delicate areas with your fingertips to keep them from lifting up. This easy circular

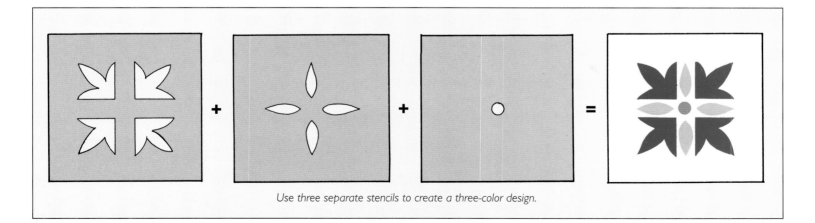

Use three separate stencils to create a three-color design.

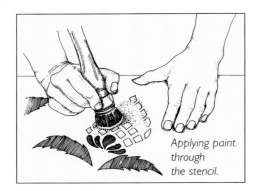

Applying paint through the stencil.

motion is the secret to beautifully stenciled interiors. Try to develop a rhythm as you work and strive for even coverage.

Sponge stenciling requires the same "almost dry" technique: moisten the sponge in water, then squeeze out all the liquid until the sponge is damp. Dip the sponge into the paint, then work off any excess by swirling the sponge on a paper plate or blotting it on a paper towel. To stencil, swirl or simply tap the sponge over the stencil cutouts.

When you are finished stenciling, release the tape and lift the stencil immediately. Allow about two minutes' drying time before taping the stencil down again to continue a border. While you are waiting, check the back of the stencil for paint seepage around the cutout edges. Moisten a paper towel with water (for

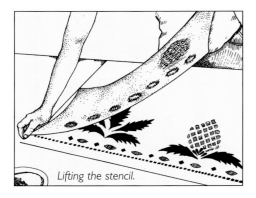

Lifting the stencil.

acrylic paints) or lighter fluid (for japan paints) and be sure to wipe off any excess. When you examine your finished work closely, you are bound to find small imperfections. Avoid the temptation to "fix" them—they are evidence of your handcrafting and part of stenciling's magical appeal.

Generally, walls are stenciled from the outside in, beginning with the borders at the frieze, then above the baseboard, down the corner joins, and around door frames and windows. This approach ensures that the borders are allotted the design space they need and that individual motifs in the open spaces are not crammed together.

Most borders can be stenciled without taking any complicated measurements: simply follow the architectural features of the room. An exception is a border with a large repeat that you want to center along the ceiling line or above the door. To do this, measure and mark the center of the space, stencil the main motif there, then continue the border out to each side for a balanced design. If you are using a multicolor design, stencil the most prominent color first in order to block out the design around the room.

Floors are best stenciled from the center out following a premarked grid. Working with a partner, stretch two strings diagonally from corner to corner to find the center of the floor area (A). Next, stretch a chalkline (a thin cabled cord *lightly* dusted with powdered dressmaker's chalk) straight across the center of the room from baseboard to baseboard (B). As you and your partner hold the line taut, have a third person verify the placement from different angles. Since the walls may not be perfectly framed, especially in older homes,

it's best not to rely on measuring for confirmation. When you are satisfied with the position, lift the line and let it "snap" against the floor to leave a mark. Measure out from this marked line to snap adjacent parallel lines, then snap perpendicular lines across the room to create the grid. A variation on this method that allows you to make adjustments after the grid is plotted is to run lengths of contrasting thread or cord across the surface and tape down the ends.

To create the look of wallpaper without borders, mark the wall as you would a floor. Find the center of the wall with diagonal cords, then drop a plumb line through the center to find the true vertical. A plumb line, sold at hardware stores, consists of a heavy weight, or bob, attached to a strong, thin cord. When the cord is suspended, the weight of the bob draws it taut in a straight line. You can snap a chalkline or run a thread alongside the plumb line to mark your first guideline.

Cleaning Up

- Latex gloves
- Soap and water
- Mineral spirits or paint thinner
- Plastic paint bucket
- Paintbrush spinner
- Rags
- Old bath towels

When you are finished stenciling, clean your brushes and sponges promptly to prolong their useful life. Acrylic paints wash off easily in cool to warm water as long as the paint is still moist. To wash a brush, rub soap into the palm of your

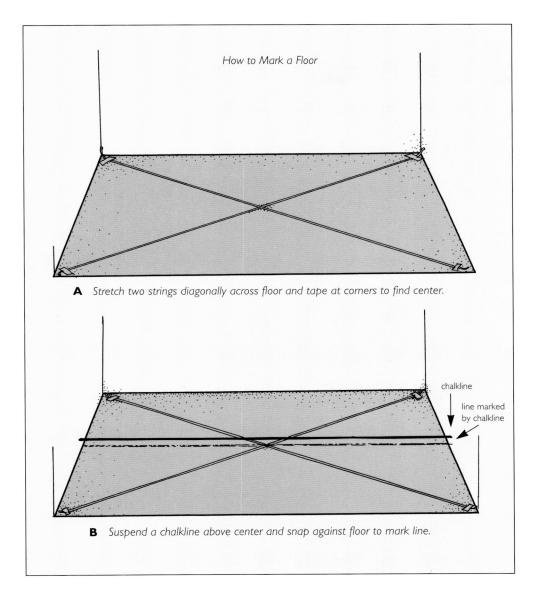

How to Mark a Floor

A *Stretch two strings diagonally across floor and tape at corners to find center.*

chalkline

line marked
by chalkline

B *Suspend a chalkline above center and snap against floor to mark line.*

ough cleaning, you can spin the remaining residue off the bristles with a brush spinner. This ingenious gadget, sold at paint and hardware stores, works like a child's hand-pumped spinning top. Be sure to point the brush down inside a paper grocery bag to contain the spray when you spin. When you are finished spinning the brush, wash out any remaining residue in warm, soapy water. Clean japan paints from stencils using a rag dipped in solvent, then follow up with a soap-and-water bath.

When you finish washing your brushes and stencils, lay them flat on toweling to dry. The dirty solvent left over from your cleaning should be recycled. Pour the solvent into a clean glass jar, screw the cover on tightly, and set the jar in an out-of-the-way place where it won't be disturbed. In one or two weeks' time, the pigment will settle and adhere to the bottom of the jar, leaving behind clear solvent ready to pour off for reuse.

The following chapters illustrate the many design options stenciling offers for home decor. You will see traditional stenciling in New England homes; stenciling by contemporary artists depicting imaginary gardens, garlands, ribbons, and animals; and bold, graphic stenciling that encourages experimentation with shape, color, and pattern. As you explore decorative stenciling, you are sure to discover new possibilities that are right for you and your home. When you are ready to take stencil brush in hand and apply that first spot of color through your hand-cut stencil, don't hesitate. Let go, take the plunge, then bask in the glorious results.

hand and swirl the bristles in the lather as if you were stenciling. Keep washing and rinsing until all the pigment has been removed. Acrylic paint that has hardened on stencils should peel right off. Paint that has crusted and hardened on a brush can sometimes be loosened and removed with toothpaste, which contains mild abrasives.

To clean japan paints, you must use a solvent, such as mineral spirits. Work outdoors or in a well-ventilated area, and wear latex gloves to protect your hands. Pour a small amount of solvent into a plastic paint bucket and recap the original container. Holding the bucket on an angle to pool the solvent, dip the brush bristles into the solvent, then press the bristles against the inside wall of the bucket to release the pigment. Repeat the process until most of the pigment is removed or dissolved. For a thor-

Country Stenciling

THE NEW ENGLAND TRADITION

The bustling but unpretentious communities and surrounding farms of early nineteenth-century New England were home to some of the most brilliant stencil art ever contrived. When a village homemaker or farmer's wife wanted something a bit fancy for her parlor, her thoughts invariably turned to allover wall stenciling, which mimicked expensive hand-blocked wallpapers imported from Europe. Most of the stenciling at this time was done by itinerant artisans who traveled about for part of the year and returned home when farming and other occupations beckoned. As professional stencilers, they packed powdered pigments, brushes, and stencils cut from oil-saturated paper, which could be rolled up for travel. Choosing stencil patterns and colors and planning each room was a shop-at-home family affair, for the stenciler boarded with each household he visited, trading gossip from neighboring and distant towns over the several days that it took him to finish the job.

Many of the nineteenth-century patterns revived for use today are credited to itinerant stenciler Moses Eaton, whose paint box and stencil kit, found in an attic in the twentieth century, have provided many important clues to early decorative stenciling. Yesteryear's most

~

Left: A key factor that makes historic stenciling so charming—and so easy to duplicate—is the guileless ease with which it overlooks perspective and realism. Even the most gifted horticulturist would be hard-pressed to grow this miraculous grapevine that shoots out of its urnlike planter like the fairy-tale beanstalk.

~

Opposite: In older homes where rooms open onto each other, stenciling can shape the interior vista. To promote a sense of passageway from one room to the next, the open doorways in this home were bordered by stenciled vines. The fanciful artwork turns daily comings and goings into something special by making each opening the indoor equivalent of a leafy garden arbor.

15

~

popular motifs included pineapples, birds, willow trees, flowers, sunbursts, and geometric designs and borders. Popular colors included red, green, black, pink, and earth tones such as ochre, burnt sienna, and burnt umber. The housewife supplied skimmed milk or cow's blood, which was stirred into the pigments to create a thin paint similar to japan paint in its translucency. To help customers visualize a pattern, the stenciler might do up a sample under the eaves in the attic. Today's crafters can adapt this custom, using the inside wall of a closet to test registration, try out a color scheme, or practice stenciling on a vertical surface.

The adaptations for New England—style stencils are many: they look as handsome on floors, floorcloths, and quilt tops as they do on walls. Authentic patterns, including those by Moses Eaton, can be found in stenciling how-to books (see Further Reading on page 70 for several titles). Designs based on geometric shapes, such as diamonds, circles, and bars, can be readily enlarged and copied from photographs in magazines, books, and museum publications. A rare but superb source is the opportunity to trace stencil patterns directly from the walls of an old house.

Traditional New England designs are especially suited to novices because their quirky, folk-art quality does not demand perfection. Unlike twentieth-century stencilers, who tend to favor precise measurements and careful calculations, nineteenth-century artisans didn't fuss over details like perfectly matched corners or evenly measured panels. More than one hundred and fifty years later, the rooms they created are still spontaneous and lively, making anyone who enters them feel he or she is on the brink of discovery.

~

Above: Middle-class colonial families enjoyed stenciling that mimicked elegant, expensive furnishings and architectural features, for it helped them express the same cultural and educational aspirations as the wealthy. In the modest dwelling viewed here, a fashionable Greek revival swag distinguishes a formal room from the workaday kitchen in the rear. In an interesting optical effect, the dangling tassels and baseboard border seem to draw together, visually lowering the ceiling. The stencil for the topmost dentil border is a very simple design of alternating thick dashes.

Right: Stenciling offers tremendous flexibility in rooms where doors and other architectural features interrupt wall space. In this old bedroom, willow trees and heart medallions find their way around a support beam, a small closet door, and the entrance door. The space above the fireplace mantel was marked into a permanent canvas for a formal willow grove. Continuous borders along the ceiling line and above the baseboard provide unity, preventing the wall stencils from appearing too disjointed.

Left: The look of old-fashioned wallpaper is easily imitated by stenciling vertical borders that divide a wall into panels. Nineteenth-century stencil artisans worked spontaneously and did not mind if the finished panels, such as those above the door here, ended up different widths. The bar-diamond border is a popular Moses Eaton design; the bars run in opposite directions on successive diamonds, giving this simple geometric art great motion and vitality.

Right: Background colors other than white can produce dazzling stenciled effects. When layers of wallpaper and paint were stripped away from the interior of an old house, this brilliant yellow wall with red stenciling emerged. The frieze border of interlocking roses runs around the room just below a white cornice, and companion rosebud borders were stenciled vertically to delineate the corner. Most of the wall surface is stenciled with a closely spaced motif that may have been intended to represent a single flower on a leafy stem.

Below: Stenciled rooms are always more lively if repeat motifs, used to pattern an entire wall surface, are interesting at close range, too. This Victorian globe lamp was stenciled with four different overlays using blue, red, gold, and black paint. The artist defied perspective by showing the front and top of the lamp simultaneously and allowing giant red posies to hover overhead.

Below: Stencils that appear "perfect" from a distance are often a composite of irregular but interesting details. A closer look at one of the dining room panels shows the quirky charm that hand cutting elicits. Of particular note are the pineapple petals, each one slightly different; the pair of feathered leaves, which affect a mirror-image pose even though they are not symmetrical; and the small diamonds lined up by twos across the top.

Above: Strict observance of historic detail decreed that no gently draping curtains could hang in this tavern-style dining room. Privacy, if needed, could be gained by closing shutters over the windows. To prevent the room from looking too angular, barren, and inhospitable, a collection of traditional stencils was created, including a pineapple, the colonial symbol of welcome.

Below: A protruding chimney wall made this green fireplace
surround and mantel all the more prominent. To preserve and
point up the symmetry, the muted yellow and green pineapple border
used throughout the room was carefully centered above it.
When the border repeat proved a bit too long to fit the space, a
small section of the pattern was circumspectly dropped out on
each side. The omission is noticeable only upon close study. The soft,
understated palette chosen for this room reflects contemporary
tastes—nineteenth-century interiors called for brighter, clearer hues.

20

Above: Painting the floorboards dark brown improved
the condition, but not the looks, of an upstairs hallway in a weekend
cottage. Just for fun, with yellow paint leftover from the closet
door and trim, traditional daisy sunbursts were added. Laid on the
diagonal, the daisies open up the space and also add an element of
safety by making the staircase more visible.

~

Below: Crisp graphic design characterizes original stenciling in this room that once served as a formal parlor. The grape clusters and swags of leaves across the top bestow blessings of prosperity and fertility upon the room. The frieze is bordered by exceptionally delicate vertical lines that show the stencil artisan's sensitivity to fine detail. In contrast, bold, closely spaced diamonds plummet the sides of the panel.

21

~

Above: The tiles selected for a country kitchen backsplash don't have to be plain white. A manufacturer's option inspired this allover traditional pattern, stenciled in olive green and golden yellow to show off a rock maple butcher-block countertop. The pattern offers great flexibility, as tiles can be added or deleted to suit almost any space configuration. The two wood catchall boxes provided smooth surfaces for trying some miniature stencil designs.

~

PART TWO

Flights of Fancy

STENCILS THAT MAKE BELIEVE

To enter a room that has been magically transformed into a garden or a palace is to engage one of life's most precious gifts: imagination. To create private worlds of escape, fun, or quiet serenity begins with a journey into the soul, as we search for those surroundings that call out to us and make us feel at home.

Many of today's most gifted decorative artists have turned to stenciling to bring their ideas for imaginative interiors to fruition. Pictorial rather than graphic in nature, their motifs include delicate rambling vines, soft floral cascades, seashells, ribbons, scrollwork, birds, and angels. Stenciling can also be used in playful ways to simulate grand architectural details: columns, moldings, chair rails, ornamental plasterwork, ancient Greek and Roman friezes, cornices, and mosaic floors. The boxy rooms, tray ceilings, and open stairwells of contemporary houses provide ready canvases for these faux looks. In children's rooms, stencils can reflect personal interests and hobbies or hint at an adventurous and challenging life in the circus, on a ranch, or in outer space. When you embark on stencil designing for a youngster's room, ask the child to help you and make the endeavor a family project.

Because of their pictorial qualities and, in some cases, mural-like size, fantasy stencils can take longer to design and cut than other motifs. The stenciling can actually go faster, though, since the stencil doesn't have to be moved around as much. Some artists work in oil paints, which dry more slowly than traditional stencil paints but offer more opportunities for color-blending and subtle shading. These marvelous details offer rich decorative beauty, and if you are interested in creating your own fantasy room, it doesn't cost much to try.

~

Left: A seemingly live and squawking hen makes a bold escape right out of her wire cage. This active chicken was stenciled with quick brushstrokes that show off the coarse texture of the plaster wall background.

23

~

~

Opposite: The decorating goal for this living room was a tall order—to establish a soft, understated ambience without altering the dark blue and white Art Deco fireplace surround original to the house. The solution: oversized sea ferns that envelop the room from floor to ceiling. Their gently undulating motion provides a soothing backdrop for the geometry of the fireplace, and the subtle ochre and pea green palette supports rather than competes with the intense colors of the tile.

Right: The butler's pantry off a large kitchen features a long, narrow passageway made even more cavernous by a high ceiling. To counteract the strong horizontal and vertical lines imposed by the cabinets and furniture, stenciled laurel branches crisscross their way along the creamy white floor. Angling the design helps to open up the space visually, and the garden theme coordinates handsomely with the botanical prints arranged on the walls. Guidelines for laying the stencils were easily marked by taping lengths of contrasting thread to the floor.

24

~

Left: Plain white walls and woodwork are spectacular in sunlit rooms, but without natural daylight, they can look dingy. This interior was rescued from a nasty case of whiteout oblivion by a lush green vine. The stenciling wends its way around the room, turning the upper door frames, which are particularly vulnerable to gloomy shadows, into leafy garden bowers.

25

~

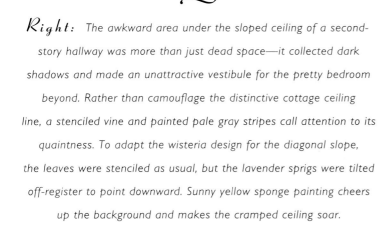

Right: The awkward area under the sloped ceiling of a second-story hallway was more than just dead space—it collected dark shadows and made an unattractive vestibule for the pretty bedroom beyond. Rather than camouflage the distinctive cottage ceiling line, a stenciled vine and painted pale gray stripes call attention to its quaintness. To adapt the wisteria design for the diagonal slope, the leaves were stenciled as usual, but the lavender sprigs were tilted off-register to point downward. Sunny yellow sponge painting cheers up the background and makes the cramped ceiling soar.

~

Left: Any plain accessory with a smooth, hard surface is a candidate for stenciled decoration. This inexpensive painted mirror frame was serviceable but offered nothing distinctive to the decor. Just a few stenciled ribbons and sprigs of tiger lily in the corners transformed it into a homespun version of the fancy Chippendale-style frame reflected from across the room. Extra care must be taken when stenciling such small, fine motifs to prevent the paint from smudging or smearing.

~

26

Right: Deep cobalt blue stenciling intensifies against a salmon-colored background, a vivid example of how complementary colors, opposites on the color wheel, play off each other. Once the viewer's attention is riveted by color, details take over, fooling the eye with realistic tassels and cords that invite closer inspection of two framed prints. Taking a few minutes extra time to stencil the wall area concealed by the prints ensures that the space is ready to accept new selections at a moment's notice.

Left: A library designed just for looks can still make a bibliophile feel at home. The original white walls of this small study rendered the space bare, dreary, and uninviting, but lining them with faux bookshelves capitalized on the room's cozy dimensions and perpetuated a sense of warmth and intimacy. The realistic volumes have colorful spines, title bars, and embossing. A mock screen, mimicking the mesh doors of the secretary in the foreground, safeguards the entire collection.

27

~

Below: The vast array of commercial stencil patterns is so enticing—
how can anyone choose just one? To narrow the field, canny decorators
scan a room's furniture and architectural features for motifs worth
developing. Here, delicate ribbon garlands appearing in relief on a white
overmantel suggested the continuous ribbon and bow border for the
frieze above. The stencil's lifelike details and shading were easily achieved by
applying several shades of pink paint through different overlays, while
the wall's muted tones are the result of sponge painting.

Left: In a luxurious master bathroom designed to pamper, sinking down into a tubful of suds places pretty stenciled tiles at eye level. The same thoughtful attention to detail is achieved in the shower stall at right and above the sink at left. This is a simple yet effective way to create unique visual interest and unity at the same time.

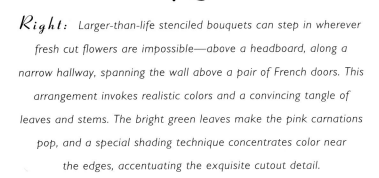

Right: Larger-than-life stenciled bouquets can step in wherever fresh cut flowers are impossible—above a headboard, along a narrow hallway, spanning the wall above a pair of French doors. This arrangement invokes realistic colors and a convincing tangle of leaves and stems. The bright green leaves make the pink carnations pop, and a special shading technique concentrates color near the edges, accentuating the exquisite cutout detail.

~

Below: Typical country-style stencils, appropriate in some settings, seemed too contrived for this family dining room with masculine overtones. A diligent search yielded the tongue-in-cheek faux herbs, hung upside down to dry. A dark stained corner molding, always something of an eyesore, became the perfect beam from which to hang them. To provide continuity, the border continues uninterrupted past the window frame.

~

Above: A stenciled vase transforms a modest front entry hall into an imaginative grand staircase. In lieu of an architectural niche in which to tuck a real vase, the classical vase was balanced on a ledge of painted molding. Several shades of taupe and gray were dabbed on the vase surface to suggest marble, and a slightly darker color brushed in along the right edge contributes realistic shading. The vase is overflowing with fresh cut flowers and a few loose tendrils of ivy.

~

Left: Painting an old parquet floor white was part of an overall remodeling scheme to lighten up a dark entry hall and kitchen. Once the job was finished, however, the white floor appeared vast and empty next to the new diamond-patterned wallpaper and curtains. To relieve the monotony without starting from scratch, rosebuds were stenciled at random across the surface. The blue ribbon that wends its way around the perimeter defines the floor plan and leads the eye toward the dining alcove, out of range on the right. A finish coat of polyurethane protects the stenciling from the inevitable scuffs of an active household.

31
~

32

Opposite: A sloped ceiling painted deep blue transforms an attic study into a fantasy nighttime observatory and adds a feeling of height. The sliver of crescent moon was added in a moment of creative whimsy using white opaque paint. Oversized white leaves flutter down a wood beam, while a line of small golden yellow blocks serves as a perpetual border to contain the expansive effect.

Above and left: Children love to make believe and appreciate deeply an environment that indulges their fantasies. With a little imagination, stencils of symbols favored by kings and queens turn an ordinary bedroom into a magic castle beckoning with adventure. Daring colors not usually chosen for a child's room—royal purple, metallic gold, orange, and turquoise—add to the drama without engulfing the space. The same paints are used to accent the thronelike chair and side table, which are thoughtfully scaled to fit a child-sized kingdom.

33

Below: The potted ivy plant sitting on top of this window bracket was so pretty, it inspired a wandering vine for the walls and sloped ceiling. The stenciling helps call attention to the pretty cottage-style architecture, while the green paint coordinates with the window treatment and ceramic pitcher and bowl. Similar allover designs can be created by using a single large stencil to cover an entire area or by cutting a collection of interconnecting smaller stencils that can be arranged freestyle in myriad permutations.

Above: Two separate motifs, one innocent and the other treacherous, trade tales in the dining room of a seaside house. Above water, a happy-go-lucky philodendron sends its dark green leaves and tendrils off to explore, reaching all the way to the room's opposite shore. A tip of the vine that made the journey waves whimsically to its reflection in a rustic twig-framed mirror. The mood changes abruptly below, where just above the gray wainscoting exaggerated ocean waves suggest stormy seas. The combination of deep natural colors, the common direction of the stencils, and the overall simplicity of the design work to unify the scheme.

~

Below: On a porch this grand (it sweeps around the house on three sides), it
was difficult to pick out at a glance the several banks of steps that led down to
the lawn. To provide courteous cues, curtains were hung above all the balustrades,
and leafy borders pointing toward the steps were stenciled around the edges
of the porch floor. In the semicircular outcropping pictured here, the stenciling
flows in a smooth arc, a shape echoed by the round table. The white and dark
green color scheme is a perennial favorite for bridging indoor and outdoor worlds.

Right: In this feminine bedroom, a peony border draws its inspiration from a printed-fabric bedspread, headboard, and canopy. As in all well-designed interiors, the eye is encouraged to wander away from the main focal point. Here, the bed's romantic, protective canopy draws the eye up toward the ceiling line, where the pretty stenciled frieze takes over, diverting attention briefly around the room. The wall basecoat was sponged in pink and white to enhance the soft feeling of the decor.

Left: A vine and tendril pattern adapted to decorate a corner looks complicated but is actually a simple repeat design about 14 inches (36cm) long. The repeat can be picked out by viewing the stenciling from left to right, comparing and matching leaves that are the same shape and located in the same position. The leaf repeats are disguised in part by the flowers, which are arranged asymmetrically in the space below and result in a natural rather than stiff effect. Several of the flowers on the two adjoining walls are identical, but because they are stenciled in different positions, the initial impression is that they are distinct designs.

Right: A close-up view of a custom-designed mirror-image corner stencil shows the subtle variations in line thickness and curves that can occur when a stencil is hand-cut. Far from being considered flaws, such distinctions lend an artistic freestyle aura to the work that commercially manufactured stencils rarely capture.

Left: Olive green upholstery fabric adorned with large peach roses inspired lively sponge stenciling on the wall behind. The rose stencil repeat, consisting of two overlapping and two individual roses, appears above the green pillow. With proper registration, the leaf stencil overlay hugs each floral grouping from above. Consequently, the top edges of the leaves appear to dance along the wall.

37

Opposite: The family that uses this large eat-in kitchen opted to dispense with a soffit, which would have enclosed the area above the hanging cabinets, and used the space to display a burgeoning folk art collection instead. To create a backdrop for their wooden figures, animals, and pint-size buildings, they stenciled a meadow of green ferns and grasses. Painting the grasses above eye level gives the entire room a cozy underground aura that recalls the storybook animal homes from The Wind in the Willows.

Below: Imaginary star flowers in various stages of bud and bloom pop up along a sinuous vine. The artist stenciled the green leaves and stems first, then added the red flowers with a light hand so the color appears to fade away. The green veins in the flowers and buds were added last.

Above: After a fresh coat of white paint brightened up this enclosed staircase, a pretend carpet runner was added to link the upstairs and downstairs decors. The stencil pattern is actually a hexagonal frieze border that was turned on end to run vertically. The Mylar stencil film was shaped to conform to the stair risers, then taped in place, just as carpet runners are secured to the treads with thumbtacks or nails. When stenciling a staircase, always work from top to bottom to avoid stepping on fresh work.

Below: An arresting chartreuse vine with pink berries was stenciled across the top of this cast-iron mantel and allowed to spill down its sides, framing the focal point of this small study and drawing attention down toward the floor and away from the room's low ceilings.

Above: A decorative folding screen is useful for warding off drafts, providing a private dressing area, or concealing a small study or home office. The leafy stenciling shown here transforms a plain white screen into a garden trellis. The trailing ivy designs are repeated in mirror image, and four different trees set in planters run down the center. To stencil the screen, it's best to remove the hinges and lay the panels down side by side so that the edges butt. The tree stencils are laid across the crack, allowing both panels to be stenciled at once.

Left: Black paint applied through a stencil of cutout squares transformed a modest white jelly cupboard into a racy accent. A close look shows that the black squares do not touch, evidence of bridges in the stencil that separate the cutout sections. The larger green and white squares on the floorcloth were painted against guidelines of white matte tape pressed onto the surface—a sort of "instant" stencil. The strawberries scattered across the floorcloth were hand-painted, though stenciled berries would have been equally as decorative. The strawberry frieze border was painted using a purchased stencil.

41

~

Right: This unusual lighted niche with a Romanesque arch suggested the covered portico of a Mediterranean courtyard garden. To cultivate the garden theme, a topiary orange tree was stenciled on the side wall in the partial shelter of the portico, its classically etched pot resting on the baseboard. To bring the tree more into the room, the leaf pattern was also stenciled into a neat border under the cornice. Note how the oranges pick up the color in the faux-tasseled drapery.

Left: An enthusiastic stenciler continued the bountiful grapes of a border stencil onto the glass panes of a Gothic window. The pointed arch makes a perfect arbor for the newly sprouted vineyard, and since the indoor window overlooks a porch addition, the paints are protected from the elements. The stenciling shows in color or in silhouette, depending on the changing light throughout the day.

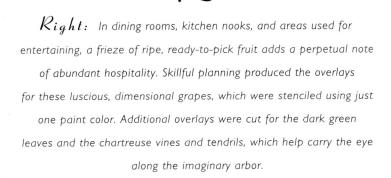

Right: In dining rooms, kitchen nooks, and areas used for entertaining, a frieze of ripe, ready-to-pick fruit adds a perpetual note of abundant hospitality. Skillful planning produced the overlays for these luscious, dimensional grapes, which were stenciled using just one paint color. Additional overlays were cut for the dark green leaves and the chartreuse vines and tendrils, which help carry the eye along the imaginary arbor.

PART THREE

Masterstrokes

ART THROUGHOUT THE HOUSE

The range for stenciled decoration in private homes has never been broader then it is today. As more and more aspects of architectural history are researched and written about, a vivid decorative past is coming to light. Artists are being called on to duplicate these designs for restoration work, while others are adapting the patterns for contemporary settings. Design sources include stencils from the late Victorian era, the turn-of-the-century Arts and Crafts movement, the Art Nouveau period, and the Art Deco period. From Europe come the highly stylized designs of the Wiener Werkstätte and the experimental farmhouse decorations of the Bloomsbury group. Other

unique sources may be found from around the world, representing a wide range of ethnic and regional motifs that tap into cultural history.

The stenciling horizon is brimming with new possibilities, such as gold metallic stars flickering down from the domed ceiling of a garden room or friendly fish swimming around a living room frieze inside an island cottage. Inspired by nothing grander than everyday scenes or a pretty picture that leaps up from the pages of a magazine, designs that fuel our own desire to create are perhaps the best of all. No longer locked into any one style, color range, or even size, people everywhere are realizing that if they can draw or trace an image and cut it out, they can stencil it. When you patiently labor over a design you love, figuring out the colors and fitting the shapes together, you exercise your mind and develop your skills and experience. This growth is the essence of creative living, and the heart of every creatively stenciled home.

Left: A pale aqua border stenciled below the cornice serves many purposes in this formal living room. In addition to closing ground on the arched interior windows and the drapery valance, the border picks up the darker teal dyes in the rug and footstool and thus maintains close ties to the floor below. Lending additional support is a companion geometric border stenciled above the baseboard. Both borders cut into the plain beige wall area, and when that wall height is "shortened," the ceiling appears less lofty.

Opposite: The problem with this niche carved out between a pillar and a closet wall was not size, but a blank dead-end wall that even artwork could not revive. Stenciling the back wall and crossbeam with primitive designs clearly defines the setback and enlivens the room.

Opposite: *A narrow border acts as an indoor horizon line, dividing a wall's pale yellow sky from its ochre earth. The border stencil for this soothing dark-to-light landscape was cut with a continuous rolling curve that emerges in ochre on the wall. Freehand pinstriping was added down the middle of the curve using a narrow brush. A pale green shadow of the border appears high on the wall just below the ceiling line, providing a sense of closure yet suggesting an ethereal presence.*

Above: *A maze of hallways and interconnecting rooms was confusing to navigate, until some stenciling color-coded the walls. In the bedroom wing hallway, ochre seemed the best transition color since the bedrooms were all different. The passage opening is framed by an informal triangle border, and a butterscotch guardian angel poses above. Beyond, in the hall off the home's reception foyer, the colors are reversed. The wall is ragged with the same pale butterscotch paint used for the angel, and an array of elegantly fragile cream-colored ferns are stenciled on top.*

~

Right: The stenciled dado
is a respectable compromise for
those who want more than
plain white walls but don't want
a totally stenciled decor. Here,
a gentle leaf and berry design
combines large stencils and
muted, low-contrast colors. The
free, windblown style suggests
the playfully irreverent decor
at Charleston, the English
farmhouse shared by Duncan
Grant, Vanessa Bell, and other
members of the Bloomsbury
group who used stenciled
motifs such as paisleys to mock
pretentious middle-class
wallpapers. The ruse is played
out here by a faux chair rail
that tastefully separates
the stenciled surface from the
plain wall above.

48

~

Below : Pale paint colors suggest an elegance that has been faded by time. Here, a light ragging produced a beige dado and lilac chair rail. Each section was stenciled individually with the same cream-colored paint used on the wall above for a finished design that looks as though it has been etched in place. To complete the exchange, a motif from the dado has been scaled down and stenciled in beige paint on the upper wall. The resulting light wash of color is perfect for showing off the lines of the deep-toned furniture and artwork.

~

Below and opposite: Stepping from the swimming pool patio's bright, hot sunshine into this dark, shaded dining room always provides welcome relief. The natural coolness of the house is enhanced by mossy earth-colored stenciling that resembles giant fossilized ferns. Innovative stencil overlays create not only the veined leaf design but also a shadowy checkerboard effect. When the walls are viewed from across the room, an oversize diamond pattern emerges. The novelty Roman lettering stenciled below the cornice is part of a quote that wraps around the room.

Right: Bathed in natural sunlight during most of the day, this almond-colored seaside kitchen sometimes appeared bland and washed-out. A stunning sailfish border stenciled around the soffit provides just the right amount of color to prevent the room from looking clinical. The folk-art vines, flowers, and curlicues surrounding the fish were stenciled through successive overlays. When a pattern involves more than two or three overlays, it helps to number them in the correct stencil order, beginning with the predominant color and ending with an accent, to avoid confusion and mistakes.

52

Left: When a white countertop meets a white wall, both lose out on any claim to distinction. Just to make clear who's who, a simple yet decorative Victorian stencil with a straight lower edge is applied to the wall just above counter level. The light brushwork is effective decoratively and prevents drips, smudges, and smears when the stencil is lifted.

~

Below: Sometimes a sleek, contemporary kitchen is secretly yearning for a warmer, more folksy, eclectic decoration. In this family-size eat-in kitchen, colorful rush-seated Mexican chairs, pillows sewn from French cottons, and hand-painted ceramicware come together harmoniously under a Victorian stenciled border and fluted glass lampshades. The scalloped stenciling mimics the fancy fretwork and shingling found on Victorian gingerbread architecture. Careful attention to registration ensures that the continuous ribbons of color meet in seamless joins around the room.

54

Left: When the same patterns and motifs keep turning up in a home, chances are there's a stencil pattern trying to emerge. Black and white checks were the hands-down favorite in this bedroom suite— checks appeared in the bed linens and dust ruffle, a woven scatter rug, and an upholstered armchair. To pick up on the theme, a double row of black squares was stenciled on a white wall, creating a bold checkered border that divides the sitting area from the sleeping alcove.

Right: Who says a library has to be dull and cheerless? The sunny disposition of this southwestern home spilled over into the office located just off the vestibule. The white bookcase walls were stenciled with bright yellow and orange paints that show Mexican scrolled ironwork designs in relief. A related design trims the bookcase edges near the room's double-door entrance. The swing-out doors are painted blue-green, a bright, happy contrast to the yellow walls and wood floor.

Left: Stencils don't have
to be in color to be dramatic.
The animal, tree, and shrub
motifs used here are shown in
crisp black silhouette against
a white wall. The designs were
adapted from assorted
photographs and drawings, then
positioned in no particular
order along a horizon line that
encircles the room. Supporting
the colorless palette are a gray
paneled dado, a framed black
and white photographic print,
and a black hammered-iron
wall sculpture.

5 5

~

Right: An unusual window treatment, consisting of pleated shades hung behind swing-open glass-paned doors, offers a master bath the twin luxuries of privacy and natural light. The look is kept fuss-free by simple light brown and olive stenciling around the window opening's wood trim. The same delicate markings decorate the front and side panels of the custom-built tub surround. The tiles and framed print pick up on the color scheme as well.

~

Below: A few carefully chosen gold accents—an ornate mirror frame, sink faucets, and stenciled fleurs-de-lis—bestow regal splendor on a contemporary white-tiled bathroom. Sparkling acrylic paint is the easiest medium for applying a precious-metals look, but for ultrarealism that doesn't pale under close inspection, try bronze stencil powders. Available in a variety of colors, the powder is rubbed through the stencil, where it adheres to a thin layer of tacky varnish.

~

Above: The same fleur-de-lis motif used on the bathroom walls enhances the doors and interior of a simple wall-hung toiletries cabinet. For fast, accurate stenciling of a border repeat, it's best to cut several identical, evenly spaced motifs side by side. To use a border stencil to paint an individual motif, such as the lone fleur-de-lis on the cabinet door, simply block off the adjacent cutout areas with tape.

~

Below: Stenciling that goes hand in hand with architectural pedigree
is always appropriate. The period border in this turn-of-the-century Arts and Crafts
kitchen features narrow interloping bands, cloverleaf swirls, and foliage
motifs, evidence of the Art Nouveau influence popular when the house was built.
Details to note include the parallel bands, repeated in the inlaid parquet,
and the graceful arches, echoed by the open door frame. To help the border fit the
space, the stenciler foreshortened the design slightly at the far corner.

Above: This stylized gray and rust border,
a succession of over a half dozen carefully plotted
overlays, created this rich interplay of designs.
In addition to using a separate stencil for each shade,
several overlays were worked in conjunction
to add the dark rust outlines surrounding each shape.
The result is a flat block-print look. The fairly
complex pattern below the chair rail, stenciled in
just one color, stands in humble contrast.

Above: Lively overlapping and a sense of
rapid, wind-blown motion obliterate the very short
repeat cycle of an Arts and Crafts–inspired
stencil. The repeat runs between the gold and brown
overlapping flowers at the upper left and
upper right of the panel section. Using overlays
to stencil scattered, free-form designs requires
meticulous attention to registration, since
there are no predictable geometric repeats to rely
on for alignment or orientation.

~

Below: *A playful, imaginative mind can base an entire decor on a single detail.
The pride of this Victorian town house parlor is the room-size carpet, lavishly
strewn with peacock feathers. They point whimsically to the stenciled border above,
where peacocks strut their plumage on endless parade between the cornice
and picture-hanging molding. This singular, theatrical room is so well put together,
it is always exciting to be in, no matter which way styles turn next.*

Left: Light streams in through this translucent glass wall, creating a magnificent luminous glow indoors. To frame this large window and prevent it from appearing institutional, stenciling fills in along the top and side supports, assuming the same positions as a valance and hanging draperies. On the crossbeam, the stencils appear in well-defined groups, unlike the same design, seen on page 44, in which the sections are butted for a smooth, seamless join.

61

Right: A collection of delicate borders mimics the wedding cake ornamentation of Victorian gingerbread houses. In older homes, designs like these can be stenciled along the wall and ceiling joins to take the place of architectural moldings, cornices, and carved wood detail. The large square design positioned in the corner of the ceiling suggests an ornamental plasterwork medallion. Because the repeats are so small, the stencil is extremely easy to set in register.

62

Left: The lines of a sinuously curved grand staircase deserve to be shown off. In earlier years, contrasting wallpaper graced entrance halls like this, setting off the white woodwork that traced the risers' upward climb. Today, the job is taken up by a broad painted band accented with stripes and floral stenciling. The dark color is practical, since the lower part of the wall is the first spot to show the dirt stirred up by foot traffic. The same design is used throughout the entry hall and can be seen face forward between the door frames under the staircase. The coordinated garland stenciling that drips from the cornice all around has been specially modified to accommodate the curved ceiling under the stairs.

~

Below: Like an exotic Mideastern mosaic, a domed ceiling shimmers with color and pattern. Each section was meticulously stenciled by an experienced artisan, who worked close to the surface by climbing up on a scaffolding. Though the work took tremendous effort to plan and execute, stenciling such a surface is still more efficient than painting a design of comparable intricacy.

63

~

Above: Almost a white elephant, an ornately carved Renaissance revival overmantel from the mid-Victorian era was an interesting, if overbearing, piece. Finding an equally strong focal point to break its dominance would allow the room's decor to develop along more eclectic lines. Enter a small, intense lotus border similar to those produced by the early twentieth-century Wiener Werkstätte. The abstract lotuses challenge the overmantel's symmetry, the warm honey and mustard hues tone down the dark wood crown, and the bright turquoise accents, small as they are, succeed in drawing the eye around the room.

Left: Native desert cacti in full bloom are an appropriate ornamentation for the stone portal of a southwestern building. The cacti rest above dark green, turquoise, and brown segments rhythmically arranged to represent a riverbed. All of the stenciling was done with brightly colored outdoor paints that can withstand harsh sun, rain, and temperature extremes.

Right: A close-up view of the cactus stenciling shows contrasting bands outlining the oval flowers and river ripples. The bands were stenciled using an overlay cut with narrow bridges. After the stenciling was completed, the blank areas covered by the bridges were painted in by hand with a small brush.

Left: String guidelines stretched across the floor ensured that these yellow and green stepped diamonds formed perfect rows horizontally, vertically, and diagonally. The four long narrow spaces in each yellow diamond correspond to bridges that join the outer stencil to its center cross motif. The large green diamonds looked the same way when initially stenciled, but then the gaps were filled in freehand for a solid look. A finish coat of clear polyurethane prevents the painted images from wear and also protects the floor surface from scuffs and scratches.

65

~

Above: When a display of flowers, pottery, or collectibles gets lost against a bare white wall, stenciled borders can help provide the necessary background. The two simple southwestern borders shown here are stenciled horizontally above a buffet. The larger, more interesting teepee border is placed on top, where it will receive the most attention, and the smaller border fills in slightly above the buffet as an anchor. Together, they function much as a picture frame does, helping to call attention to the objects that hover between them.

~

Below: An unfortunate architectural partition cut across this large room right between two doorways. To better unify the space and minimize the partition, a stepped southwestern border was stenciled just slightly below it, then continued at the same level around the room. The painted trastero and freestanding coatrack inspired the gray and orange color scheme as well as the southwestern theme.

~

Below: Gilded stars adorn the edge of a thick board shelf supported by a pair of mismatched brackets. The stenciled stars, which pick up the dark blue of the lamp and rug, provided a fun, easy way to decorate the shelf, which was put together from salvaged materials and sponged with the same light blue paint used on the low dado.

~

Above: Row upon row of ethnic designs look like part of a woven textile, but this fool-the-eye carpet was actually stenciled permanently onto the wooden floorboards. The geometric designs were worked in just a few colors, plus black and white, to let the floor's wood grain show through. To complete the deception, a realistic turned-back corner interrupts the borders at the lower left.

~

Below : Sponge painting and stenciling transform a tray ceiling—an architectural feature popular in many newly built homes—into a starry twilight sky. The sponging was done in shades of mauve, violet, and purple, coordinating subtly with the bed linens and upholstered bench and creating an eerie glow near the horizon that gradually darkens overhead. Gothic arches stenciled around the perimeter appear as footlights on this nighttime theater. When the room lighting is dimmed, tiny gold metallic stenciled stars sparkle overhead.

~

Above : A bold intarsia floor looks like parquet but is actually a creative application of paint and stain. The freestyle diamonds, each one slightly different in size, give an idea of how easy and uncalculating this design really is. The paint was applied first to create the basic stenciled gridwork of red circles and black triangular borders. When the turquoise stain was brushed into the large, open areas, the paint acted as a holding band to prevent the stain from seeping beyond the edges. Small five-pointed stars are stenciled at random on top.

Below: The golden oak flooring in this busy kitchen corridor and work area was handsome and durable, but compared to the new verdigris marble countertops, it lacked sophistication and polish. The solution: paint. A few layers of dark teal built up a strong basecoat across the entire floor surface, and to add subtle design interest, stars and triangles were stenciled at random in navy blue. The close color tones keep the floor sophisticated and avoid a spotty, cluttered look that would detract from the room's handsome architectural columns and built-in cabinetry.

Above: Most stenciled rooms develop from a master plan, but stenciling at random can be fun, too. The stars scattered above this living room's picture-hanging molding are spaced far apart and show different intensities, just as they do in the nighttime sky. The friendly serpent came into being one day, and as long as there is bare wall space, other creatures are bound to follow. Outside in the hall, another flurry of activity produced the bright red-orange maple leaves, which flutter up the stairwell as if scattered by a sudden gust of autumn wind.

Sources
~

The materials and equipment needed for stenciling, including acrylic and japan paints, Mylar polyester film, craft knives, rulers, and white matte tape, are sold at art-supply stores worldwide. Consult your telephone directory for a store near you. Many art-supply stores in larger cities offer catalog mail-order service.

Commercially manufactured precut stencils are available in home-decorating stores, mass market retail stores, hardware stores, and craft and hobby shops. Companies specializing in custom designs can be located by consulting advertisements in craft and decorating magazines.

Design ideas for stenciling abound. Pattern books written especially for stencilers are a primary source and an excellent reference for the beginner. Your public librarian can help you identify additional pictorial sources for historic, folkloric, and ethnic designs that interest you. Generally, these include books and periodicals related to the fine arts, architecture, needlework, and the graphic arts. Books on nature and the sciences can yield information and inspiration for designs featuring trees, vines, flowers,

vegetables, fruits, animals, fish, birds, shells, and other natural forms. Illustrated children's books are an excellent source for designs of many types, and you may enjoy browsing through them. Other sources include wrapping paper, greeting cards, advertising circulars, product packaging, magazines, catalogs, posters, fabrics, and wallpapers. By keeping copies of the designs you like, you can build your own personal source library.

For additional information on stenciling products, instruction, publications, seminars, and local stenciling groups worldwide, contact:

Stencil Artisans League, Inc.
P.O. Box 920190
Norcross, GA 30092
USA

Further Reading

Jewett, Kenneth. *Early New England Wall Stencils: A Workbook.* New York: Harmony Books, 1979.

Le Grice, Lyn. *The Art of Stencilling.* New York: Clarkson N. Potter, 1986.

Parry, Megan. *Stenciling.* New York: Van Nostrand Reinhold Company, 1977.

The Stenciled House: An Inspirational and Practical Guide to Transforming Your Home. New York: Simon & Schuster, 1988.

Waring, Janet. *Early American Stencils on Walls and Furniture.* New York: Dover Publications, Inc., 1968.

Warrender, Carolyn, and Tessa Strickland. *Carolyn Warrender's Book of Stencilling.* New York: Harmony Books, 1988.

Conversion Chart for Common Measurements

~

The following chart lists the approximate metric equivalents of inch measurements up to 20", rounded for practical use. To calculate equivalents not listed, multiply the number of inches by 2.54cm. To convert 36", for example, multiply 36 times 2.54, for an equivalent of 91.44cm, or 91.5cm when rounded.

½" = 1.3cm	
1" = 2.5cm	11" = 28cm
2" = 5cm	12" = 30.5cm
3" = 7.5cm	13" = 33cm
4" = 10cm	14" = 35.5cm
5" = 12.5cm	15" = 38cm
6" = 15cm	16" = 40.5cm
7" = 18cm	17" = 43cm
8" = 20.5cm	18" = 45.5cm
9" = 23cm	19" = 48cm
10" = 25.5cm	20" = 51cm

Photography Credits